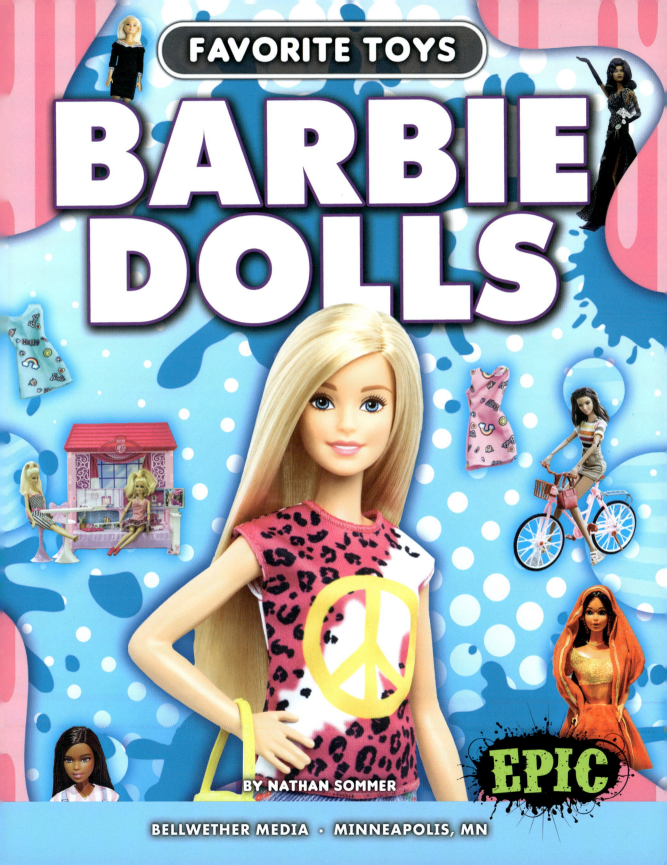

Favorite Toys
BARBIE DOLLS

BY NATHAN SOMMER

BELLWETHER MEDIA • MINNEAPOLIS, MN

EPIC

EPIC

Action and adventure collide in **EPIC**. Plunge into a universe of powerful beasts, hair-raising tales, and high-speed excitement. Astonishing explorations await. Can you handle it?

This is not an official Barbie book. It is not approved by or connected with Mattel, Inc.

This edition first published in 2022 by Bellwether Media, Inc.

No part of this publication may be reproduced in whole or in part without written permission of the publisher. For information regarding permission, write to Bellwether Media, Inc., Attention: Permissions Department, 6012 Blue Circle Drive, Minnetonka, MN 55343.

Library of Congress Cataloging-in-Publication Data

LC record for Barbie Dolls available at: https://lccn.loc.gov/2021044256

Text copyright © 2022 by Bellwether Media, Inc. EPIC and associated logos are trademarks and/or registered trademarks of Bellwether Media, Inc.

Editor: Elizabeth Neuenfeldt   Designer: Josh Brink

Printed in the United States of America, North Mankato, MN.

TABLE OF CONTENTS

A Day With Barbie................. 4
The History Of Barbie Dolls .. 6
Barbie Dolls Today 14
More Than A Toy 18
Glossary 22
To Learn More........................23
Index......................................24

A Day With Barbie

A girl plays with a Barbie doll. First, Barbie goes to work. Then she dances with friends in the Barbie Dreamhouse.

Barbie ends the day camping outside. Barbie dolls are full of endless fun!

BARBIE DREAMHOUSE

A FAMOUS DOLL

BARBIE DOLLS ARE THE BEST-SELLING FASHION DOLLS IN THE WORLD. THEY ARE SOLD IN 150 COUNTRIES!

The History of Barbie Dolls

Ruth Handler created Barbie dolls in California in the 1950s. She was an owner of the toy company Mattel.

Ruth wanted to make Barbie dolls to show girls they can do anything!

RUTH HANDLER

BARBIE DOLL BEGINNINGS

Los Angeles, California = ●

1959 BARBIE DOLLS

The first Barbie doll **debuted** at the 1959 New York Toy Fair. It came with blonde or brown hair.

Barbie dolls were popular right away. Around 350,000 Barbie dolls sold in their first year!

BEHIND THE NAME

THE BARBIE AND KEN DOLLS WERE NAMED AFTER RUTH HANDLER'S TWO CHILDREN.

1961 KEN DOLL

1963 MIDGE DOLL

Mattel soon created friends for Barbie dolls. Ken dolls debuted in 1961. Midge and Skipper dolls came next.

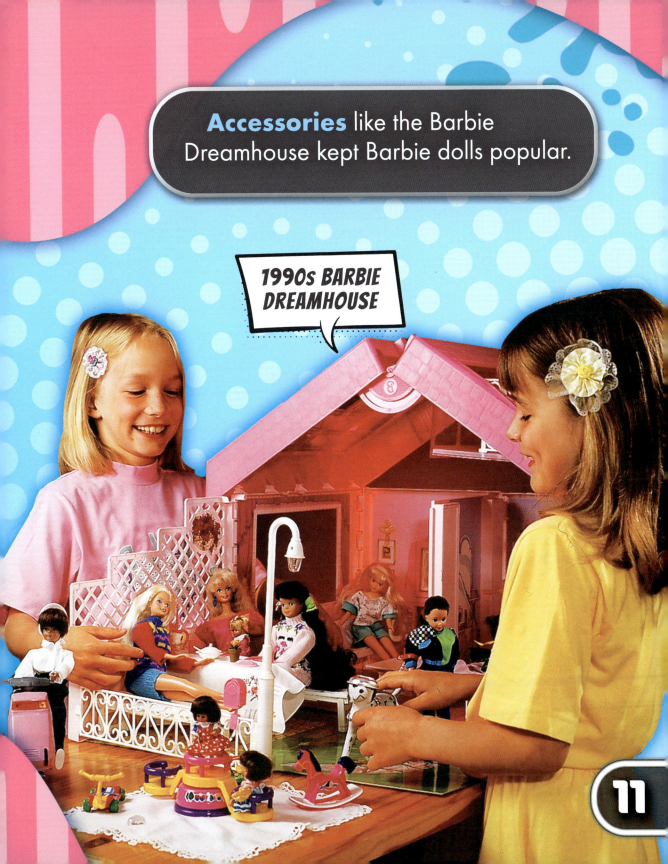

Black and Hispanic dolls named Barbie debuted in 1980. Mattel created their first doll with a **disability** in 1997.

Barbie dolls with different body types debuted in 2016. Kids of all backgrounds can see themselves in a Barbie doll!

2016 BARBIE FASHIONISTAS DOLLS

BARBIE DOLL TIMELINE

1959
The first Barbie doll is shown at the New York Toy Fair

1961
The Ken doll debuts

1980
Mattel debuts the first Black and Hispanic dolls named Barbie

1997
Mattel makes their first dolls with disabilities

2016
Barbie dolls with different body types are made

Barbie Dolls Today

Many Barbie dolls have fun **careers**. Dolls have been teachers and firefighters. There is even a President Barbie doll! Barbie Role Models look like famous women in history. They **inspire** girls around the world!

2020 BARBIE ROLE MODELS

BARBIE DOLL TYPES

Malibu Barbie

Barbie Role Models

Totally Hair Barbie

Breathe with Me Barbie

15

Many adults who grew up with Barbie dolls still collect them. Barbie dolls based on movies are popular **collectibles**.

MILLIONS OF BARBIE DOLLS

MORE THAN 100 BARBIE DOLLS ARE SOLD EVERY MINUTE. MATTEL SELLS AROUND 58 MILLION DOLLS EVERY YEAR!

The dolls continue to see strong sales worldwide today!

More Than A Toy

Barbie doll fans attend **conventions**. They stay in touch through **social media**. Fans also visit museums. The Barbie **Expo** in Montreal has more than 1,000 different Barbie dolls!

BARBIE EXPO

BARBIE EXPO PROFILE

Where Is It? Montreal, Quebec, Canada

What Is It? The largest museum collection of Barbie dolls in the world

When Did It Start? 2016

Barbie dolls star in many movies and video games. Fans watch *Barbie Dreamhouse Adventures* on Netflix.

SO MANY MOVIES

THERE ARE MORE THAN 30 BARBIE DOLL MOVIES! FANS ENJOY MOVIES LIKE *BARBIE IN ROCK 'N ROYALS* AND *BARBIE PRINCESS ADVENTURE*.

BARBIE IN ROCK 'N ROYALS

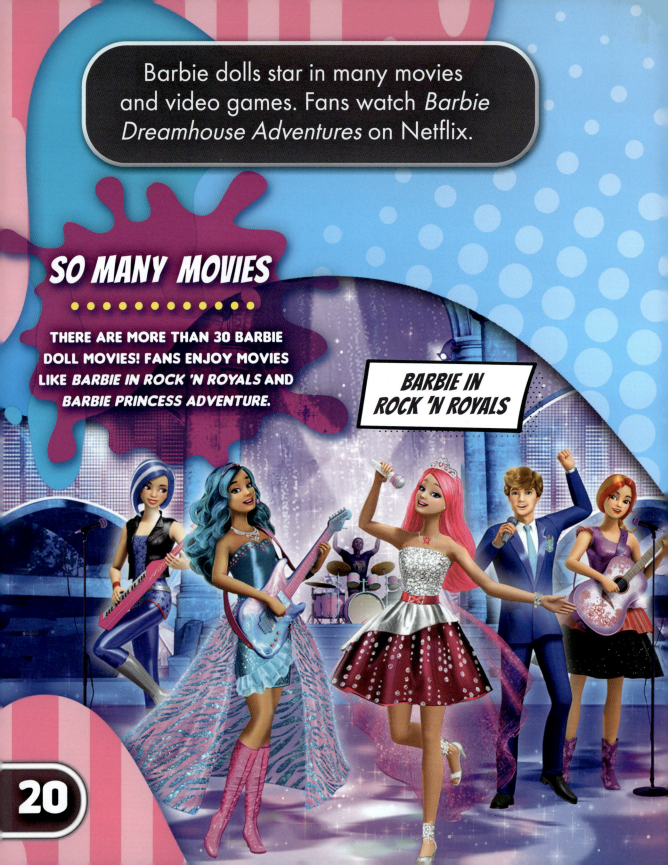

20

Barbie dolls are fun to play with and watch. They have inspired kids and adults for more than 60 years!

Glossary

accessories—items added to something else to make it more useful or attractive

careers—jobs that people do for a long time

collectibles—items that are seen as valuable

conventions—events where fans of a subject meet

debuted—was shown to the public for the first time

disability—something that limits a person's ability to move, talk, or sense

expo—a place where collected items are shown

inspire—to give someone an idea about what to do or create

social media—websites where people can share information, ideas, messages, photos, and videos

To Learn More

AT THE LIBRARY

Bowman, Chris. *Action Figures*. Minneapolis, Minn.: Bellwether Media, 2022.

Eagan, Cindy. *The Story of Barbie and the Woman Who Created Her*. New York, N.Y.: Random House, 2017.

Loh-Hagan, Virginia. *Girl Innovators*. Ann Arbor, Mich.: Cherry Lake Publishing, 2020.

ON THE WEB

FACTSURFER

Factsurfer.com gives you a safe, fun way to find more information.

1. Go to www.factsurfer.com.

2. Enter "Barbie dolls" into the search box and click 🔍.

3. Select your book cover to see a list of related content.

23

Index

accessories, 11
Barbie Dreamhouse, 4, 11
Barbie Dreamhouse Adventures, 20
Barbie Expo, 18, 19
Barbie in Rock 'n Royals, 20
Barbie Princess Adventure, 20
Barbie Role Models, 14
beginnings, 7
body types, 12
California, 6
careers, 14
collectibles, 16
conventions, 18
disability, 12
Handler, Ruth, 6, 10

history, 6, 7, 8, 9, 10, 11, 12
Ken, 10
Mattel, 6, 10, 17
Midge, 10
Montreal, 18
movies, 16, 20
museums, 18
name, 10
New York Toy Fair, 8
profile, 19
sales, 5, 9, 17
Skipper, 10
timeline, 13
types, 15
video games, 20

The images in this book are reproduced through the courtesy of: Mattel, Inc. front cover (hero), pp. 2 (left, right), 4, 5, 7 (left, middle, right), 8 (left Barbie), 10 (Midge, Ken), 12-13 (all), 14-15, 15 (Malibu Barbie, Barbie Role Models, Totally Hair Barbie); AlesiaKan, front cover (Barbie top left, blue and pink dresses), pp. 4-5 (child); Catherine Zibo, front cover (Barbie Expo Barbie), back cover (bottom right), p. 19 (left, right); Sean P. Aune, front cover (bottom left Barbie), back cover (top right, bottom middle), p. 15 (Breathe With Me Barbie); NeydtStock, front cover (Barbie on bike), back cover (top left); Suphatthra olovedog, front cover (Barbie doll house); siempreverde22, front cover (bottom right); DinosArt, back cover (bottom left); Brenda Rocha - Blossom, p. 3 (Barbie on bicycle); REUTERS/ Alamy, pp. 6, 9; ZUMA Press, Inc./ Alamy, p. 8 (right Barbie, box); dpa picture alliance archive/ Alamy, p. 16; iswannawi, p. 17; picturelibrary/ Alamy, p. 18; IgorGolovniov, p. 19 (logo); AP Images, p. 21.